HOW TO KEEP A SECRET

Writing and Talking in Code

Elizabeth James & Carol Barkin

Illustrations by Joel Schick

Lothrop, Lee & Shepard Company

A Division of William Morrow & Co., Inc. • New York

For Big David, Little David, and Spike

Library of Congress Cataloging in Publication Data
James, Elizabeth.
   How to keep a secret.

   SUMMARY: Presents various methods of writing, speaking, and signaling secret
messages.
   1. Ciphers—Juvenile literature.   2. Cryptography—Juvenile literature.   [1. Ciphers.   2. Cryptography]   I. Barkin, Carol, joint author.   II. Title.
Z103.3.J35   001.54′36   77-18295
ISBN 0-688-41828-7
      0-688-51828-1 lib. bdg.

Contents

Noitcudortni

Wouldn't it be great to be able to talk to your friends without anyone else knowing what you're saying? Just about everybody uses codes to keep secrets. Do you remember people spelling in front of you when you were really little and they didn't want you to know what your birthday present was? That's one way of talking in code. Of course, that won't work any more because you can spell too. But maybe you spell out w-a-l-k when your dog is around because he can't.

You probably know about some other kinds of codes. If you heard someone say "Smokey's on the move, good buddy," you might recognize the CB radio way of saying "There's a police car coming, pal." Or if you turned on the tv and heard a voice say, "Ten-four, car six," you'd know right away that someone was using the police call code. Because so many people know what they mean, these codes aren't very secret any more.

Different groups of people have used various kinds of codes to communicate secretly with other members of the group. In the Old West, Indians used smoke signals to send coded messages over long distances. Outsiders saw the smoke

5

but didn't know what it meant. Hoboes used to use chalk symbols on houses to tell other hoboes what to expect—a large, mean dog, or a good chance of a free meal. Even in your own family you might use secret words or phrases in front of "company" that only members of your family understand.

Sometimes codes may be used not to keep secrets, but as a kind of shorthand that can be understood by everyone. International traffic signs use simple pictures or symbols that can be understood all over the world, no matter what language people speak. If you are a Scout, you may have learned how to read trailblazing signs in the woods. This code gives all hikers information about the trail. And almost everyone knows what "roger," "wilco," "over," and "out" mean. These two-way radio code words are easy to speak and to understand even when reception is poor and crackly.

All kinds of groups have developed secret ways of recognizing each other or communicating. People have used secret handshakes, passwords, signals, and even code tattoos!

You probably have a group of pals who always do things together. Maybe you'd like to form a club and invent your own secret language. And what about code names for the club's members? You could use CB-style names, like "Rubber Duck," or invent code names based on one of the codes in this book.

In this book you will find many different kinds of secret spoken and written languages. After you understand how they work, you can make up some secret codes of your own that only you and your friends will understand. For a start, try decoding the heading on page 5.

Secret Spoken Languages

How would you like to share your secrets with your friends right out loud? If you could speak a secret language, you wouldn't have to whisper—other people might hear you but they wouldn't know what you were saying!

Pig Latin is one kind of secret language. Here's how it works.

1. For words that begin with a single consonant, move the beginning consonant to the end of the word and add "ay" at the end.

"Tom needs help" becomes "Omtay eedsnay elphay."

2. For words beginning with more than one consonant, move the whole beginning consonant group to the end of the word and add "ay" at the end.

"Spies bring trouble!" becomes "Iesspay ingbray oubletray!"

3. For words beginning with a vowel (or vowel sound) leave the word as is and add "way" to the end of it.

"Emergency action! I am alone" becomes "Emergencyway actionway! Iway amway aloneway."

The trouble with Pig Latin is that an awful lot of people can understand it. The only way to keep Pig Latin messages secret is to practice it all the time with your friends—then you'll be able to speak it too fast for other people!

See how fast you can say this Pig Latin message. Then decode to find out what Tom is supposed to do.

"Omtay, elltay usway ouryay ocationlay."

Here's what Tom replies:

"I'mway idinghay inway away Inesechay estaurantray!"

Then Poppy radios new instructions to Tom from the clubhouse:

"Avesay ecretsay essagemay! On'tday eatway ortunefay ookiecay!"

Did you notice how peculiar Pig Latin sounds? This is partly because all the words begin with vowels and also because of the repeated "ay" sound.

If too many people around you know Pig Latin, try one of the other secret languages. Have you ever heard of "Egg" or "Opp"? They work a little differently from Pig Latin. And they sound even sillier. You just add an extra syllable ("egg" or "opp") before each vowel sound of every word.

In "Egg," Peggy would be Peggeggeggy. Poppy would be Peggoppeggy.

But in "Opp," Peggy would be Poppeggoppy. And Poppy would be Poppoppoppy.

And now back to our story.

8

Teggom's geggot beggad neggews. "Peggeggeggy steggole thegge feggorteggune ceggookeggie!"
"Stoppop hopper!" shoppouts Poppoppoppy.

To keep your secrets really safe, make up your own secret language using the rules of Egg and Opp. You can use any new syllable you want. For an Egg language, use a vowel followed by a consonant sound—how about "ick"?
Decode the rest of Poppy's message to Tom:

"Quickick! Ickafticker hicker! Fickollickow thicke fickortickune cickookickie!"

You can also use the rules of Pig Latin to make up a new secret language. Choose a vowel sound for the ends of the words. Just be sure to use an extra consonant for words that begin with vowel sounds.
See if you can figure out how Tom's new secret language works:

Omtoo andzoo Oppypoo aysoo, "Eesoo ouyoo inzoo Apterchoo Otwoo."

(Did you figure out that the secret sounds are "oo" and "zoo"?)

Secret languages like Pig Latin, Egg, and Opp are just ordinary English words rearranged, so it's pretty easy for outsiders to catch on to what you're saying. If you were a spy, you wouldn't want to take this chance! A good way to solve this problem is to use code words. The best part about this is that you and your friends can choose any code words you like and decide what you want them to mean. Then the only way your code can be broken is if one person tells what the code words stand for.

Here's how code words can baffle an unwanted eavesdropper. Suppose you suspect that your bratty little brother or sister is listening in on your phone call to your friend. If you and your friend have agreed on this code:

bratty little brother or sister = math book
going to the movies = doing special homework

your conversation might sound like this:

You: What time are we meeting to do our special homework tonight?
Friend: Seven o'clock. Are you supposed to bring your math book?
You: No. Luckily I don't have to drag that along.

Your sister or brother would never suspect a thing!

Of course, you could always use words like "you know what" and "you know who" to disguise your meaning. But then your brother or sister would know right away that something fishy was going on. The whole point of code words is to choose natural-sounding ones so that other people won't realize you don't mean what they think you do. That's really keeping a secret!

Sometimes it may not matter if other people know you're talking in code. Then your code words can be as crazy as you want. You and your friends may go around talking about a purple elephant and sticky green monsters instead of your gym teacher and the members of another secret club. Or you could make up your own words. Try using an acronym—a word formed from the first letters of a group of words. A very well-known acronym is:

SNAFU = Situation normal, all fouled up.

You could use an acronym of club members' initials for the name of your secret club; Kathy, George, Robert, Allan, Linda, and Sue might form a club called the GLARKS. (You may need to stick in extra vowels if all the words start with consonants! If your mother calls you and your buddies The Terrible Three, your club could be called TOTOT.)

Then how about a secret password acronym for your club? Only open the door for people who knock three times and whisper "HAND"! (Did you guess that HAND is an acronym for "Have a nice day"?)

Think up some really wild ideas; try making an acronym of your favorite song or any expression your group uses all the time. Do you constantly say "What a weird idea" or "Tough luck on you!"? These would make great passwords—WAWI and TLOY.

You can change your password or the secret language you use as often as you want. Just be sure your pals all get the secret message. Then you'll always be able to talk to each other out loud, on the bus or in the halls, without checking beforehand for spies!

HAND!

Transposition Ciphers

Think of all the times you wish you could write in a secret language! Notes passed to friends may fall into the wrong hands; a letter to a pal may be read by nosy little brothers; the secrets in your diary may be opened to the world!

An easy way to disguise what you're writing is to run all the words together without any spaces or to break them up with spaces in different places. Can you read these space ciphers?

TOMISHOTONPEGGYSTRAIL
PEG GYST IL LHA STHEFO RTU NECO OKI E!

Both of these methods, however, are very easy to decode. They're just a handy way to keep outsiders from reading your messages at a glance.

Written secret languages are divided into codes and ciphers. In a code, whole words are substituted for the original words or phrases; this is like the spoken code words on page 10. In a cipher, the letters of each word in a secret message are rearranged or replaced. However, it is convenient to call any kind of disguised writing a code.

Using code words may sound a lot easier than changing each individual letter. But unless you only need to write a few key words in code, you'll soon find that your list of code words and their meanings is as long as a dictionary! Remember, there are only 26 letters in our alphabet but there are thousands of words in our language.

In the easiest kinds of ciphers, the letters of the original message are not changed—they are just rearranged, or transposed. You've probably used a transposition cipher without even knowing that's what it was; have you ever written anything backward? This is the backward cipher:

S'MOT OIDAR SELKCARC. "HCIHW YAW SI YGGEP GNIOG?" SKSA YPPOP.

It's harder to decode backward cipher if you put the words in backward order too.

MOT SEILPER, "OOZ EHT ROF GNIDAEH S'EHS."

And it gets even trickier if you change the spacing in your backward message and take out all the punctuation.

TNA TROP MI SIEI KOO CENU TROFT AH TYP POPS YA SREHES OLT NOD

If your name is Anna or Hannah, don't sign your messages in backward cipher—you'll see why if you try it! Words or phrases that are spelled the same backward as forward are called "palindromes." You may have heard what Adam said to Eve when he met her: "MADAM, I'M ADAM." She held out her hand and replied simply, "EVE."

14

Backward cipher is easy to do—but unfortunately it's also easy for anyone to figure out. The key to backward cipher— reading it backward—is not very hard to spot. Fencepost cipher is a transposition cipher that's much more difficult to decode unless you know the key to it.

Here is how to write a message in fencepost cipher. Write your message on two lines, putting the first letter on the top line, the second letter on the bottom line, the third letter on the top line, the fourth letter on the bottom line, and so on. Don't leave any spaces—just run the words together.

ATEOPGYUKITTEETLHUE
THZOEGDCSNOHRPIEOSB

(If your message has an odd number of letters, add a dummy letter to the end.)

To encode your message, write the top line followed by the bottom line. Break it up into fake words to make it more confusing.

ATEOP GYUK ITTE ETLHU ETHZO EGD CSNO HRPI EOSB

Send your coded message to your friend, and don't forget to destroy your working copy. When your friend receives your message in fencepost cipher, all she has to do is divide the message exactly in half. Then she writes down the first half and writes the second half directly underneath it. Now she can read your message—she will know that the dummy letter at the end should be ignored.

If you want to make triple-sure that the wrong people can't read your message, use taller fenceposts! On your working copy, write your message on three lines instead of two.

TFLSTGHVIELOEALAS
OOOBPGAASDLMERIRK
MLWUEYSNHATSSEZDL

dummy letters

To encode the message, write the top line, then the middle line, and then the bottom line. Use spacing to look like words, and then destroy the working copy to keep your message secret.

16

TFLS TGH VIELO EALA SOOOB PGA ASDL MER
IRKM LWU EY SNHATS SEZDL

. . .

Sign your secret message with three dots—this will tell your
friend how many equal sections she or he should divide the
message into. Then she or he just has to write the first section
on one line, the second section below it, and the third section
on the bottom line.

Any number of lines can be used in the fencepost cipher.
See if you can decode this:

TENAO SUEL EGR FOAOS OTH HTAI SYOTR
CMN WTEE SNMP INHI ADT WODS IDP ENTELG
OKHD AO DGS GFOGLE

. . . . .

(Did you notice that this message has no dummy letters?)
Here is the last message you will receive in Chapter 2:

MSED NP TEOET ECTH BRCCS HER YER OIAREE

. . . .

Alphabet Substitution Ciphers

Do you suspect that spies have cracked your code? Are your secrets being found out by the wrong people? Maybe your transposition cipher is too easy to decode. It's time to try a new way of keeping your secrets safe.

Substitution ciphers, unlike transposition ciphers, don't use the actual letters of the original message. As you've probably guessed, a new letter or other symbol is substituted for each letter in the message. So unless you have the key, these codes are a lot harder to break.

The simplest substitution cipher is the backward alphabet cipher. To encode a message in this cipher, write out the English alphabet and then write the alphabet backward above it; Z goes over A, Y over B, etc. This is your code alphabet.

code alphabet⟩

Z Y X W V U T S R Q P O N M L K J I H G F E D C B A◀⟩
A B C D E F G H I J K L M N O P Q R S T U V W X Y Z

Now you can write a message in the backward alphabet cipher. Here's a message to practice decoding.

GSV TLIROOZ RH HNRORMT ZG KVTTB. "LS, ML!"
GSRMPH GLN.

(You can leave out all the punctuation in your messages if
you want to make them harder to figure out.)

Once someone finds out that you're using the backward
alphabet cipher, you're in trouble! This is why some secret
agents use an alphabet shift cipher that needs a key. The code
alphabet is shifted forward any number of letters you decide
on. Here is the simplest shift:

code alphabet

Z A B C D E F G H I J K L M N O P Q R S T U V W X Y

A B C D E F G H I J K L M N O P Q R S T U V W X Y Z

SNL'R QZCHN BQZBJKDR. "SGHR HR
GDZCPTZQSDQR. VGZS'R
GZOODMHMF?" ZRJR ONOOX.

Of course, you can shift forward any number of letters you
want. And you can change this key number every week or even
every day. Superman liked this code so much that he used it
for messages to members of his secret club. (Captain America
uses it too.) Superman's Secret Code had nine different key
numbers:

Code Mercury: shift 1 B=A
Code Venus: shift 2 C=A
Code Mars: shift 3 D=A
Code Jupiter: shift 4 E=A
Code Saturn: shift 5 F=A

19

Code Uranus: shift 6 G=A
Code Neptune: shift 7 H=A
Code Pluto: shift 8   I=A
Code Krypton: shift 9 J=A

(Code Earth, of course, was plain English!)

If you're shifting more than one or two letters, try this easy way of encoding and decoding messages. Write the alphabet once on graph paper or between the lines of notebook paper turned sideways to keep all the letters spaced evenly; this is your code alphabet. Then make a long strip of the same kind of paper with 52 spaces. Write two normal alphabets, one after the other, on this coding strip. Then when you line up the A on the long coding strip with its code letter, you will always be able to see the corresponding letters at both ends of the alphabet.

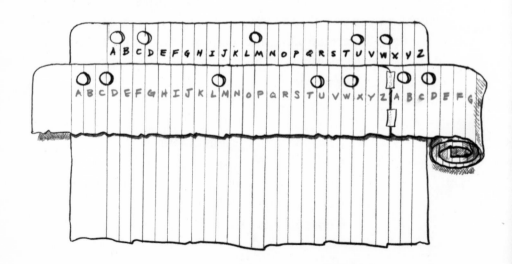

Devise your own system to tell your partner what key number you are using. You might base it on days of the week: shift forward 1 letter on Monday, 2 letters on Tuesday, and so on. Or use the months of the year and shift forward 1 letter in January—by December you'll shift forward 12 (M=A). Here's a way to make your alphabet shift cipher really tough to crack. Write the letter of your code alphabet that corresponds to A at the end of the first word of your code message, or any other place you and your partner agree on. Try decoding this message: the key letter is at the end of the first word.

"RJ LJW'C UXXT! R'V JOAJRM CQN PXARUUJ JCN CQN OXACDWN LXXTRN!" LARNB CXV.

(Remember to leave out the punctuation marks when you write your coded messages to make them harder to crack.)

For top secret messages you can combine the backward alphabet and the alphabet shift ciphers! Don't forget to write your code alphabet backward before deciding on your key number (you can use the coding strip you used for regular alphabet shift). If your key number is six, A=T, B=S,

code alphabet

T S R Q P O N M L K J I H G F E D C B A Z Y X W V U

A B C D E F G H I J K L M N O P Q R S T U V W X Y Z

C=R, D=Q, etc. Make sure your partner knows that you're using backward shift cipher as well as the key number. You can arrange to use a different signal for the key number in each kind of cipher; for backward shift cipher you might write your message so it takes up the same number of lines as the

21

key number you're using. Try that system to decode this
message:

FGFFW DURMGC TUSK,
"U OGGR RQBQSBMZQ
IUKQC CADQ GP
BNQ PUSBC. TQBBQD
SNQSK MB GAB."

(Did you notice that in this cipher the letter K corresponds
to K in the coded message? If your key number is odd, the
two alphabets will always meet somewhere; with an even
key number no letters are the same.)

Is the name of your club a secret? Or do you have a secret
password? You can make a fancy kind of alphabet shift
cipher using this secret word. This is called the key word
shift.

For your code alphabet, write the key word and then the
rest of the alphabet, leaving out the letters that are in the
key word. The key word here is "spycode."

code alphabet

S P Y C O D E A B F G H I J K L M N Q R T U V W X Z

A B C D E F G H I J K L M N O P Q R S T U V W X Y Z

Make sure your key word has no repeated letters ("secret"
won't work, for instance). And choose a word with one or
two letters that occur fairly late in the alphabet; otherwise the
last letters of the code alphabet will be the same as the regular
alphabet (Y is good to have in your key word because then
only Z is the same in both alphabets).

22

Try decoding this message (the key word is "spycode").

RK IQJOS GQTLKJ LOE EXA OQB JH TY GRA
ODK NRT JOYK KGB OBQQRB HHBJ A ONAS JC

Notice how much harder the message is to read with both punctuation and word spacing taken out. This is just another spycode trick!

DKNIKNORNBYGQRTNJRAOLSEO
(SPYCODE)

Number Substitution Ciphers

Does one member of your club have terrible handwriting? Are his or her messages getting garbled because you can't read the letters? Switch to number substitution ciphers!

All the alphabet substitution codes can be done in numbers instead. Of course, the easiest number substitution code is a number alphabet cipher, in which A=1, B=2, C=3, and so on. You can use the same coding strip you made for alphabet substitution ciphers. But your "code alphabet" will be the numbers 1 through 26.

20-15-13-7-18   1-2-19-16-5   7-7-25-8-1   14-4-15-22-5
18-20-8-1-20   6-15-18-20-21   14-5-3-15-15
11-9-5-9-20   19-20-8-5-15   14-12-25-15-14   5-12-5-6-20
9-14-20-8-5   23-15-18-12-4

If you divide your message into groups of five numbers each, it won't be so easy to see where words begin or end. Fewer clues for spies!

To do number shift cipher, choose a key number (instead

of a key letter) and shift your coding strip so that A is directly under your key number. Then encode your message. Be sure you always put dashes between the numbers of your message or your partner will not know whether he should read "fifteen" or "one, five." Confuse the enemy, not your partner!

Don't forget that you have to tell your partner what your key number is. Sign a fake name at the bottom of your message; the number of letters in the name is your key number.

12-1-3-3-21 15-23-21-15-5 23-9-23-3-21
12-15-21-23-10 26-9-21-25-14 21-15-16-23-8
24-23-8-8-5 15-24-14-11-7 1-10-5-9-17
15-16-4-23-18 1-16-4-1-25 11-11-7-5-1
16-11-16-1-8 8-2-11-14-16 17-10-1-15

Mortimer Aloysius Bean, Esq.

(Be sure to count all the letters in the fake name. Did you figure out that A = 23?)

Of course, you can also do backward alphabet and backward shift ciphers in numbers. Or try a key name shift cipher. Letting A = 1, write out the alphabet in numbers. Then, on a strip of paper, write down the numbers that spell out your name or your club's name, followed by the numbers for the rest of the alphabet (leaving out the ones you've already used).

A B C D E F G H I J K L M
1 2 3 4 5 6 7 8 9 10 11 12 13

N O P Q R S T U V W X Y Z
14 15 16 17 18 19 20 21 22 23 24 25 26

If your club name is WOLVES, your code strip will be:

W O L V E S A B C D F G H
23 15 12 22 5 19 1 2 3 4 6 7 8
A B C D E F G H I J K L M

I J K M N P Q R T U X Y Z
9 10 11 13 14 16 17 18 20 21 24 25 26
N O P Q R S T U V W X Y Z

When you write the alphabet in normal order under these numbers, you can use the numbers to encode your message. You can see that each letter will have a different number every time you change the key word.

Here's another installment of The Fortune Cookie Mystery for you to decode. (Hint: This is a key name shift and my name is Sherlock, so the number code looks like this:

19 8 5 18 12 15 3 11 1 2 4 6 7
A B C D E F G H I J K L M

9 10 13 14 16 17 20 21 22 23 24 25 26)
N O P Q R S T U V W X Y Z)

20-10-7-12-24   13-6-19-1-9   17-20-11-1-17
15-10-16-20-21   9-12-5-10-10   4-1-12-5-10
9-20-19-1-9   17-20-11-12-6   10-9-3-6-10
17-20-17-12-5   16-12-20-16-12   5-1-13-12-15
10-16-15-10-16   20-21-9-12-5   10-10-4-1-12
17-23-11-12-9   1-20-1-17-16   12-20-21-16-9
12-18-20-11-12   16-12-23-1-6   6-8-12-7-1
6-6-1-10-9   17-10-15-15-10   16-20-21-9-12
5-10-10-4-1   12-17

26

Are you ready to try something different? With the co-ordinates cipher you'll finally find a good use for all that graph paper you got for math class.

Draw a 5 × 5 grid and write one letter of the alphabet in each square (Y and Z can share a space). Number the squares along the top and left side. Then, for each letter of your message find the two coordinate numbers; be sure to use the number along the side first and then the one on the top.

Here's how this cipher key looks:

	1	2	3	4	5
1	A	B	C	D	E
2	F	G	H	I	J
3	K	L	M	N	O
4	P	Q	R	S	T
5	U	V	W	X	Y/z

ANT = 113445

Since each letter has two numbers, you don't have to use dashes between them. But you may want to add spaces and dashes to confuse people and keep them from guessing what cipher you're using.

Here is a message in coordinates cipher:

```
2434  4523  1145  1311  4415  2414  3534  4534
1515  1424  4544  1155  4441  1522  2255  4423
1523  1134  1444  4523  1521  3543  4551  3415
1335  3531  2415  4535  4535  3355
```

When you write your code message in groups of four or five numbers, be sure to make a complete group at the end

—use dummy numbers. This makes it harder for people to know what code you're using.

If an enemy spy suspects that you are using the coordinates cipher, double your security! Write the alphabet in the grid in a different order (up and down or backward) or don't use any order at all—just make sure your partner has a copy of the grid you're using. Or try using different numbers along the top and sides. Experiment with different ways of camouflaging your communications.

	1	2	3	4	5
5	Y/z	P	O	F	E
6	X	Q	N	G	D
7	W	R	M	H	C
8	V	S	L	I	B
9	U	T	K	J	A

	5	4	3	2	1
1	B	J	O	I	K
2	P	H	L	T	A
3	E	G	M	S	U
4	V	R	N	C	F
5	Q	Y/z	W	D	X

An even better way to disguise your cipher is to use a different shape of grid. You can combine I and J (or W and X or P and Q) in one space for a 6 × 4 grid.

	1	2	3	4
1	A	B	C	D
2	E	F	G	H
3	I/J	K	L	M
4	N	O	P	Q
5	R	S	T	U
6	V	W	X	Y/z

Or make a larger grid—leave the extra spaces blank for dummy numbers or put in punctuation marks like ? and !

	1	2	3	4
7	A	C	F	J
6	B	E	I	N
5	D	H	M	R
4	G	L	Q	V
3	K	P	U	Y
2	O	T	X	?
1	S	W	Z	!

	1	3	5	7	9
1			!	?	Z
2	M	L	K	J	Y
3	N	C	B	I	X
4	O	D	A	H	W
5	P	E	F	G	V
6	Q	R	S	T	U

Do you have trouble remembering the number key for the code you're using? Are you constantly calling your partner on the phone (which may be tapped!) to find out the key for decoding the last message? If so, the telephone cipher is the one for you! You're not very likely to forget your own phone number, or your partner's—and those are the keys to this cipher.

The telephone cipher works completely differently from the other ciphers in this chapter. Here's how you do it. Write out your message and then write the seven numbers of your phone number over the first seven letters. Keep writing the digits of the phone number over each letter until you reach the end of the message.

Phone number: 802-7312

802 73 1 2802 73128 02731 2802 731
"You're a good sport, Peggy," says Tom.

To encode your message, work with one letter at a time. Shift the first letter forward the same number of places in the alphabet as the number above it: in this case, shift Y forward 8 places, to become G. Continue to shift each letter forward the number of places written above it. (Of course you can change the spacing so it doesn't look like words.)

Here is the above message in telephone code:

GOWYH BIWOF ZSPTB PGNJZ UIYUA R̲N̲K̲L̲F̲ ⤺
dummy letters⤷

To decode, write the phone number the same way over the letters of the code message—then shift *backward* the number of places written above each letter.

30

Try decoding this installment of The Fortune Cookie Mystery; the phone number is 802-7312.

BOOYD EKWSR VSQAU IUZLP PICEV PQNQS
JLGUJ MFQYW VPMCQ VNJGQ SUHIF

The beauty of the telephone cipher is that each letter has a different code letter every time (unless your phone number is something like 444-4444!). This makes the code practically uncrackable without knowing the key number. Of course, it takes a little more time to encode and decode than some of the others, but that's the price you pay for top security!

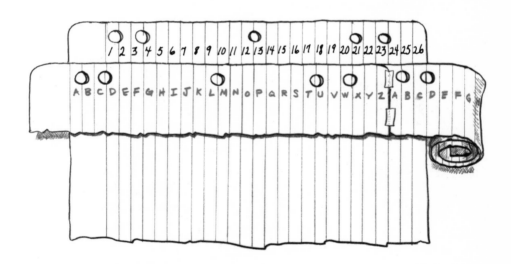

Secret Alphabets

You might already know a "secret" alphabet—one that does not use letters or numbers to stand for the original letters of a message. Do you know what this famous signal means?

$$\cdot \ \cdot \ \cdot / \_ \ \_ \ \_ / \cdot \ \cdot \ \cdot$$

Of course, Morse code is not a *secret* alphabet, since the purpose of it is to help people communicate easily. A ship broadcasting S-O-S does not want this to be a secret message!

Still, if no one in your neighborhood besides your club members knows Morse code, it can be a great way of sending secret messages. And you can send them in so many different ways! You can write down the dots and dashes (make slashes to keep the letters separate). You can use a flashlight or even a window shade. If you saw three short, three long, and three short flashes coming from the basement, you'd know that your partner had been captured by the enemy—or that your father had painted himself into a corner!

Better yet, you can use sound to send Morse code messages: a pencil tapping on your desk may sound like fidgeting when

you're really sending a message that only one person in your class understands.

The international Morse alphabet looks like this:

Try decoding this message:

--·/---/---/-··/·--/---/·--/·-·/-/·---/--/···/·-/

_·--/···/·--·/---/·--·/·--·/·-··/·/·-/-/-/····/·/

_··-·/---/---/-·-/··/·/-···/···-/-/···/·-/··· -/·/-/

····,/·/··· /·/·/-·-·/·-·/·/-/

Morse is easy to learn and easy to use. You can have a lot
of fun talking in Morse to all kinds of people. But remember
that it is an international code language—it's not a good way
to keep secrets!

Don't despair—your secrets can still be safe. There is another well-known secret alphabet called Pigpen or Tic-tac-toe.
It has been used for centuries and you might wonder how it
can still be secret. The trick is to arrange the letters for coding
in your own individual way.

Here's an example of how Pigpen works.

AZ	DW	GT
BY	EV	HS
CX	FU	IR

JQ

MN   KP

LO

To write the alphabet in Pigpen, draw the compartment
each letter is in with or without the dot. The above version
of the Pigpen alphabet looks like this:

A B C D E F G H I J K L M

N O P Q R S T U V W X Y Z

You can see that the letters could be arranged in the compartments in any order you like. (Just make sure your partner knows which order you're using!)

Use the Pigpen alphabet above to decode this message:

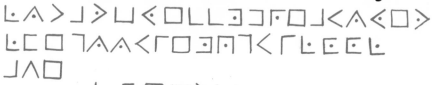

It's fun to make up your own secret alphabet. There are lots of possibilities, such as circles with lines through them or other geometric figures. Or just make up your own squiggly scratch marks or hieroglyphics to represent the letters of the alphabet. (Has your teacher told you lately that your handwriting is really a secret alphabet?)

Warning: be sure your copy of your secret alphabet is kept safe under lock and key. Who knows where spies may lurk?

Secret Coding Devices

People may wonder why all the members of your club walk around with pieces of broom handles sticking out of their back pockets. What these people don't know is that the broom handles are really secret coding devices!

Coding devices are fun to use and many are simple to make. Coding sticks can be made from almost any cylinder—toilet paper or paper towel cores, candles, or broom handles. The important point is that everyone in your club must have one exactly the same size.

Here's what you do. Cut a long, narrow strip of paper and wrap it around your coding stick in a spiral. The margins (blank edges) of newspapers make terrific code paper. But of course strips of any other paper will do.

When you wrap the coding paper around your coding stick, make sure the paper overlaps a bit to form a solid paper surface all the way across. (You may need to anchor the ends with masking tape.) Then just write your message across the overlapping edges of the paper. (Ballpoint or fine-line felt tip pens work best.) When you unwrap it, the long strip of paper is covered with meaningless squiggly marks. But when your partner wraps it up on his stick the message reappears! And if a spy gets hold of your code paper message, he won't be able to read it unless he has a coding stick exactly as thick as yours.

If carrying around a coding stick lets too many people know you are passing secrets, you may want to use a coding key that you can keep hidden in your wallet! Coding keys are easy to make. Just draw a square on a sheet of paper: make the sides 6 cm. long. Mark six equal spaces on each side. Write the alphabet around the outside of the square, putting one letter in each space (double up I/J and Y/Z). Now cut out a square the same size from a piece of light cardboard

(the back of a writing tablet is perfect). Make the same letter spaces, this time on the inside edge of the square. This cardboard square is your coding key, so you will write the letters on it in random order. Make an arrow pointing to one side of the square.

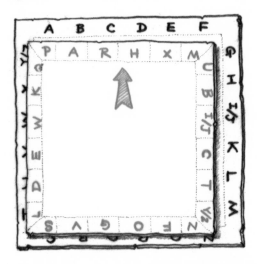

To encode a message, put the coding key over the alphabet square with the arrow pointing up. Find the first letter of your message on the alphabet square and write down the code letter that corresponds to it. Using the coding key shown, write the message "Beware." The first code letter is A.

For the second letter, turn the coding key one turn clockwise and find the second letter of your message. In our message, E = K. Continue turning the coding key one turn clockwise for each new letter.

B E W A R E

A K C U V K

38

To decode, look for each letter of the code message on the coding key and find the letter that corresponds to it on the alphabet square. Don't forget to turn the coding key once for each new letter.

Once you get used to this method, encoding and decoding go very quickly. But you can see that without the coding key it would be almost impossible to read secret messages. So make sure that everyone who is authorized to read them has an identical coding key!

You can vary your codes by using a triangle with equal sides instead of a square. A good size is 11 cm. on each side. You will make 9 equal letter spaces and leave a blank space at each end where it's too hard to write. Since $9 \times 3 = 27$, you will have one extra space; use it for a ? or ! or any other symbol. Make the arrow point to a corner of the triangle, and use this coding key just like the square one.

You may want to experiment with other geometric shapes for coding keys. Just make sure that all the sides are equal in length, and that you put the same number of letter spaces on each side.

If your coding key is captured by enemy agents, don't worry. Put your school books to good use—they make great coding devices! Here's how a book code works. Look through your book to find the first word you need for your message. Write down the page number where it appears. Then count down from the top of the page to find the line number (ignore titles and subtitles) and write this number after the page number. Finally, count in from the left margin until you reach the word you need and write this word number after the line number (a partial word at the beginning of the line counts as a whole word). Use dashes to keep the numbers separate and be sure your partner has the same edition of the book that you do.

Read the following coded message using this book:

13-5-7-22-11-3-17-15-9

Of course you never mark the words in your book—what if it fell into the wrong hands?

Are your friends getting a little bored playing cards on rainy afternoons? Here is a fantastic new use for regular playing cards—and it doesn't involve marking the deck!

Each person who sends a message in playing card code will need his or her own deck. In this code each suit is used for one kind of information.

Here's one way you could do it:

Each person in the group chooses a face card for a signature card. Yours might be the Jack of Diamonds or the Queen of Hearts or whatever one you like. Since there are 12 different face cards in every deck you might have some that aren't assigned to anyone. You could use them for some other meaning. Then let Clubs stand for the days of the week, Diamonds for the time of day, Hearts for the place, and Spades for information and directions.

Clubs: days of the week
Monday = ace	Friday = 5
Tuesday = 2	Saturday = 6
Wednesday = 3	Sunday = 7
Thursday = 4	

Diamonds: time of day

1 o'clock = ace	6 o'clock = 6
2 o'clock = 2	7 o'clock = 7
3 o'clock = 3	8 o'clock = 8
4 o'clock = 4	9 o'clock = 9
5 o'clock = 5	10 o'clock = 10

11 o'clock = any two diamonds that add up to 11
12 o'clock = any two diamonds that add up to 12
AM = 8 of Clubs
PM = 9 of Clubs
Overnight = 10 of Clubs

Hearts: place
at my house = ace
at your house = 2
at clubhouse = 3
at school = 4
at movie theater = 5
at playground = 6
at park = 7
at sports field = 8
at bus stop = 9
at the Y = 10

Spades: information and directions
phone me = ace
meet me = 2
bring food = 3
bring money = 4
pass on to other members = 5

meeting = 6
party = 7
homework = 8
Okay = 9
No, can't do it = 10

Any joker = Emergency!

Suppose you open your locker at lunchtime and see an envelope containing these cards. What would they mean in the above playing card code?

3 of Clubs
5 of Diamonds
9 of Clubs
5 of Hearts
2 of Spades
4 of Spades
Jack of Clubs

Or what about this one?

6 of Hearts
4 of Diamonds
9 of Clubs
5 of Clubs
6 of Spades
5 of Spades
Joker
Queen of Hearts

(The decoded messages are on page 56.)

Naturally you and your friends can get back the cards you gave out for messages the next time you get together. Or maybe someone will pass those cards back to you in a message.

There are lots of ordinary objects that can make good coding devices. Something as simple as sticking a pencil be-hind your ear can be a signal to your friends. Or you could make an elaborate code system with colored marbles. Make your code device as simple or complicated as you like.

Invisible and Secret Writing

Do you worry about your messages being intercepted? Wouldn't it be great to be able to send postcards that only your partner could read? Use invisible writing to send a secret message between the lines of an innocent-looking greeting! No one will ever suspect that "Wish you were here" has a hidden meaning!

The simplest kind of invisible writing is pressure writing. You don't need any special equipment, so you can do it in the middle of the desert or on a sinking ship.

You need a ballpoint pen or a pencil that is not too sharp. Lay a piece of scratch paper over the paper you want to write your message on. Press down hard as you write on the scratch paper: this pressure will make indented writing on the message paper underneath. For best results, put a writing pad or a magazine under your message paper while you write.

Spies will notice right away if you and your friends pass around a seemingly blank piece of paper. Disguise your secret message by writing it between the lines of regular writing on a letter, notebook page, or other ordinary piece of writing. To position the pressure writing correctly, use onionskin or other lightweight scratch paper—this way you can see what's under the scratch paper as you write.

To read pressure writing, hold the paper at an angle under a light bulb. Tilt the paper until the light hits it just right and makes the letters show up. For privacy, use a flashlight at midnight under the covers!

If you can use a typewriter, you can do pressure typing. Insert two pieces of paper in the typewriter. When you type on the top one, the pressure makes indented letters on the second sheet. (Be sure to destroy the top sheet when you're finished!)

Pressure typing is sometimes too easy to read, even without a slant light. To avoid revealing your secrets, type your messages in code. Then your message paper will appear to have a lot of random letters indented on it, as if a lot of people had used it behind their typing paper! Only your partner will know that this beat-up paper contains an important message.

The indentations of pressure writing can be felt on the back of the paper, so if a spy with sensitive fingertips has been handling your secret messages, you may want to switch to watermark writing. All you need is two sheets of paper, a ball-point pen or blunt pencil, a hard surface to write on (such as a Formica counter top or glass table top), and plain water. Wet one sheet of paper on both sides and lay it flat on your writing surface. Lay the dry sheet on top of it and write your message on it—press very hard. Let your message paper dry, and the secret message will completely disappear!

Disguise the "blank" message paper with a fake message written in light pencil—you can go right over the watermark writing. Or make it into a paper airplane and sail it at your partner!

To develop a watermark message, just run water over both sides of the sheet of paper. As soon as the paper is wet, the message will appear!

Remember: for pressure writing use a soft writing surface to make indented letters; for watermark writing write on a hard surface so the letters *won't* be indented.

Breakfast time is best for composing messages in invisible "ink"—using *milk!* On fairly soft paper (file cards and news-

46

paper work very well), write with a toothpick or a very small paintbrush dipped in milk. Keep track of where you're writing—the letters are invisible as you write them!

Now you will need some powdered pencil lead (from a small hand pencil sharpener) or powdered ashes. Sneak outside and get some from the barbecue, or take a little from the fireplace: put the ashes in an envelope, tape down the flap with masking tape, and label it "Developing Powder." To develop the invisible milk message, dip your finger in the powder and rub it over the paper where the writing is. The words will appear like magic! (Remember to wash your hands afterward so no one will know what you've been doing.)

Here's a quick way of sending short messages in invisible milk ink. Tear out a small piece from a newspaper and underline the words you need for your message with milk (write one or two extra words in the margin if you need to). Your partner can develop the message by smearing developing powder over the whole piece of newspaper—the underlines and any words you've written will show up clearly. Conserve the supply of developing powder: keep this message small!

The best part about milk ink is that it doesn't require any hard-to-find chemicals and you don't need strong heat to develop it. There is another very easy way of sending messages in secret writing.

If you are being held captive with nothing but a newspaper to read and the safety pin that's holding your shirt together, you can get a secret message out to your friends in pinprick writing! Use the pin to make a line of pinholes in the newspaper under each word you need for your message. Your captors will never notice the pinpricks, but when your friends hold the newspaper up to a light, they'll see your cry for help right away. To make the message easier to decode, make one pinhole above the column where your message starts, two holes above the second column you use, and so on.

If you're desperate and you can't find a word you need, you can write the letters out with pinpricks in a blank space or in the margin. Don't do this often, though—it's much easier for spies to spot pinprick words than to see the underlining.

You can probably think up some other kinds of secret writing. A popular method is mirror writing—the message is written backward so it can be read when held up to a mirror.

Mirror writing is easy to learn; you will quickly find that you can print backward without using a mirror to help you. But it's also quite easy to read, so to keep your secrets safe you should do your mirror writing in code. The mirror writing will just be an extra precaution to keep snoopers out. And for absolutely top secret information, try *invisible* mirror writing—in code!

Keeping Things Secret

If your secret partner passes you in the hall and whistles a few bars of "Mary Had a Little Lamb," don't jump to the conclusion that he's lost his marbles! He's probably signaling to you that he's left a secret message in your locker.

On the other hand, if a member of your club hums "Pop! Goes the Weasel" in the lunchroom, conceal your secret papers! She's warning you that a weasely spy is lurking nearby.

There are thousands of ways to send secret signals. You can tie your scarf in different ways: put the knot in front for "Danger" and on one side for "All Clear," or untie it and knot it again for "Pick up a message." Of course you can always signal by scratching your head (or your elbow). But you can get a little fancier by using your partner's full name instead of his usual nickname or by saying "Hello, there" instead of "Hi." Get together with your partner and work out a system of signals using ordinary words and gestures. Just make sure they're not too obvious—you don't want every spy in the neighborhood to know you're sending secret signals. And you don't have to be elaborate: something as simple as handing your partner a book wrong side up can signal that you've put a message in the book, or that you've left one in your secret hiding place.

A secret spot where code messages are dropped off and picked up is called a "drop." You will probably want to have several message drops: if you always use the same one, you're likely to be found out. A good place is the reference section of the library, since those books can't be checked out. Pick a book that is rarely used (look for a dusty one) and put your code message between the pages. Even if other people run across it, they won't understand what it says and they'll probably leave it where they found it. A loose corner of carpet can also be a handy indoor drop, but watch out for spring cleaning days!

If you know your partner's locker combination, you can wad up the message and push it halfway down her jacket sleeve; she'll find it when she puts on her jacket to go home. Or, in the gym locker room, try stuffing it into the toe of her left tennis shoe.

A message drop is only useful if it's a place where both partners can go without arousing suspicion. You may have some convenient outdoor drops, such as under a rock (use a plastic bag to protect your message) or in a bush or a hollow tree. However, if none of these are available, or if they've been discovered, try wadding up the message and sticking it into a prearranged hole of a chain link fence. Choose a hole near the ground to avoid detection—your message will look like a piece of litter! Another drop that's too obvious for rival clubs to check is a community bulletin board. Grocery stores, churches, and community centers often have notice boards that anyone can use: tack up your messages there in plain sight.

Look for other public places to use as message drops. One of the best drops is a pay phone booth. It's open all the time to anyone; it's protected from the weather; you can go in any time without arousing suspicion (make a fake call to preserve your camouflage); it's small enough to be completely private.

Carry a roll of tape with you at all times. Then you can tape a message to the bottom of the phone or under the shelf. For larger messages or other secret items, try using a brown paper lunch bag. The one your lunch was in is fine, because it is prewrinkled! Scrunch up the bag with the message inside

and leave it in a corner of the phone booth. Most people will think it contains an apple core or a half-eaten baloney sandwich and they won't touch it; only your partner will know it's important.

You may want to mark your paper bag so your partner will know it's the right one. Use a secret signal such as a hole punched with a pencil or a triangle torn out of the top edge.

Has someone ever rummaged through your desk drawer looking for a ruler and accidentally come across all your code sheets? Take precautions! Find some secret hiding places in your room so you can keep all your code information safe. Who would ever bother to look in a big manila envelope labeled "Math Tests from 4th Grade" or at the bottom of a box of old doll clothes? Give some thought to choosing your hiding place. Your mother may decide to clear out that very dresser drawer for a rummage sale, or your brother may borrow the exact book or record you've hidden your code sheets in.

Look around your room for really unusual places. Tape or pin a code sheet to the back of your curtain at the side edge. Or pull out a desk or dresser drawer and tape secret information to the bottom. (Make sure the drawer still slides smoothly so your secrets won't be discovered!)

Does the front edge of your dresser rest directly on the floor? If so, there is a terrific and extra-large secret space under the bottom drawer. Just pull the drawer all the way out; you can store everything you need for keeping secrets here.

Keep on the alert for new and different hiding places. Then, as you learn each new code, you'll have a place to stash the coding keys and secret messages.

And now, a final important message:

SGGDI UJNHS QDJID IQADO PJJFD OQJKO LYNLQ
KSOOJ IJIGX QJSRQ AJNDZ LCKLN OJIOW

(This is a key word shift cipher; the key word is **SPYCLUB**. See page 22 for help in decoding this message.)

Codes Decoded

THE FORTUNE COOKIE MYSTERY

Chapter 1

page 7: Tom needs help.
 Spies bring trouble!
 Emergency action! I am alone.
page 8: "Tom, tell us your location."
 "I'm hiding in a Chinese restaurant!"
 "Save secret message! Don't eat fortune cookie!"
page 9: Tom's got bad news. "Peggy stole the fortune cookie!"
 "Stop her!" shouts Poppy.
 "Quick! After her! Follow the fortune cookie!"
 Tom and Poppy say, "See you in Chapter Two."

Chapter 2
page 13: Tom is hot on Peggy's trail.
 Peggy still has the fortune cookie!
page 14: Tom's radio crackles. "Which way is Peggy going?" asks
 Poppy.
 "She's heading for the zoo," replies Tom.
 "Don't lose her," says Poppy. "That fortune cookie is important."
page 16: At the zoo, Peggy ducks into the reptile house.
 Tom follows but Peggy has vanished! All Tom sees are
 lizards.
page 17: Tom doesn't know what to do. He dashes outside and
 glimpses Peggy in front of the gorilla cage. More secret codes
 in Chapter Three. Bye.

Chapter 3
page 19: The gorilla is smiling at Peggy. "Oh, no!" thinks Tom.
 Tom's radio crackles. "This is headquarters. What's hap-
 pening?" asks Poppy.
page 21: "I can't look! I'm afraid the gorilla ate the fortune cookie!"
 cries Tom.

page 22: Poppy radios back, "A good detective makes sure of the facts. Better check it out."

page 23: Tom sneaks up on Peggy. He's in luck! The fortune cookie is still in her hand.

For more tricks turn the page.

Chapter 4

page 24: Tom grabs Peggy. "Hand over the fortune cookie! It's the only one left in the world."

page 25: Peggy says, "I am a gypsy and my crystal ball is broken. I must have the cookie to tell fortunes."

page 26: Tom explains, "This fortune cookie contains the long lost secret recipe for fortune cookies. When it is returned, there will be millions of fortune cookies."

page 27: "In that case, I don't need it," says Peggy.

She hands the fortune cookie to Tom.

page 30: ("You're a good sport, Peggy," says Tom.)

page 31: Tom radios Poppy, "Mission accomplished! The fortune cookie is safe!"

Chapter 5

page 32: (SOS)

page 34: "Good work, Tom," says Poppy. "Eat the cookie but save the secret."

page 35: Tom and Peggy break open the cookie. Yuck, it's stale! The end.

Other coded messages

Chapter 6

page 43: Meet me at the movie theater at 5 PM on Wednesday. Bring money. (signed) Jack of Clubs

Emergency meeting at the playground Friday afternoon at 4 o'clock! Pass this on. (signed) Queen of Hearts

Chapter 8

page 54: All information in this book is top secret. Pass on only to authorized persons.